DATE:_____/_____/_____

"Change your thoughts and you change your world." – Norman Vincent Peale

NEVER
GIVE UP

DATE:___/___/___

think
positive

"The best way to gain self-confidence is to do what
you are afraid to do." – Unknown

DATE:___/___/___

MAKE IT HAPPEN

DATE: ___/___/___

think positive

"Happiness often sneaks in through a door
you didn't know you left open." – John
Barrymore

DATE:____/____/____

"Life is what we make it, always has been, always will be." – Grandma Moses

BELIEVE YOU CAN

DATE:___/___/___

think
positive

"When we are no longer able to change a situation, we are
challenged to change ourselves." – Viktor Frankl

DATE:___/___/___

"You may be disappointed if you fail, but you are doomed if you don't try." – Beverly Sills

BELIEVE IN YOURSELF

DATE:___/___/___

think positive

"If you can change your mind, you can change
your life." – William James

DATE:___/___/___

"Dream big and dare to fail."
— Norman Vaughan

TAKE ACTION!

DATE:___/___/___

think positive

"When the world pushes you to your knees, you're in the
perfect position to pray." – Rumi

DATE:___/___/___

NEVER EVER GIVE UP

DATE:___/___/___

think positive

"The next time you feel slightly uncomfortable with the pressure in your life, remember no pressure, no diamonds. Pressure is a part of success." – Eric Thomas

DATE:____/____/____

"I would rather die of passion than of boredom." – Vincent van Gogh

MAKE IT HAPPEN

DATE:___/___/___

think positive

"You must make a decision that you are going to move on. It wont happen automatically. You will have to rise up and say, 'I don't care how hard this is, I don't care how disappointed I am, I'm not going to let this get the best of me. I'm moving on with my life." – Joel Osteen

DATE:_____/_____/_____

"You become what you believe."
– Oprah Winfrey

BELIEVE YOU CAN

DATE:___/___/___

think positive

"Be soft. Do not let the world make you hard. Do not let pain make you hate. Do not let the bitterness steal your sweetness. Take pride that even though the rest of the world may disagree, you still believe it to be a beautiful place." – Kurt Vonnegut

DATE:___/___/___

"It is never too late to be what you might have been." – George Eliot

BELIEVE IN YOURSELF

DATE:___/___/___

think
positive

"Happiness, like unhappiness, is a proactive choice." – Stephen Covey

DATE:___/___/___

TAKE ACTION!

DATE:___/___/___

think positive

"Success is falling nine times and getting
up ten." – Jon Bon Jovi

DATE:_____/_____/_____

"A person who never made a mistake never tried anything new." – Albert Einstein

NEVER EVER GIVE UP

DATE:___/___/___

think positive

"All things are difficult before they are easy." – Thomas Fuller

DATE:____/____/____

MAKE IT HAPPEN

DATE:___/___/___

think positive

"You are never too old to set another goal
or dream a new dream." — C.S Lewis

DATE:___/___/___

"Limitations live only in our minds. But if we use our imaginations, our possibilities become limitless." – Jamie Paolinetti

BELIEVE YOU CAN

DATE:___/___/___

think positive

"The difference in winning and losing is most often...not quitting." – Walt Disney

DATE:___/___/___

"Too many of us are not living our dreams because we are living our fears." — Les Brown

BELIEVE IN YOURSELF

DATE:___/___/___

think positive

"When I do good, I feel good. When I do bad, I feel bad. That's my religion." — Abraham Lincoln

DATE:___/___/___

TAKE ACTION!

DATE:___/___/___

think positive

DATE:___/___/___

"Start where you are. Use what you have. Do what you can." – Arthur Ashe

NEVER EVER GIVE UP

DATE:____/____/____

think positive

"There is little difference in people, but that little difference makes a big difference. The little difference is attitude. The big difference is whether it is positive or negative." – W. Clement Stone

DATE:___/___/___

MAKE IT HAPPEN

DATE:___/___/___

think positive

"If someone tells you, "You can't" they really
mean, "I can't." – Sean Stephenson"

DATE:___/___/___

"The only person you are destined to become is the person you decide to be." – Ralph Waldo Emerson

BELIEVE YOU CAN

DATE:___/___/___

think positive

"The difference between stumbling blocks and stepping stones is how you use them." – Unknown

DATE:___/___/___

BELIEVE IN YOURSELF

DATE:___/___/___

think
positive

"We are responsible for what we are, and whatever we wish ourselves to be, we have the power to make ourselves." – Swami Vivekananda

DATE:___/___/___

TAKE ACTION!

DATE:___/___/___

*"I am the greatest, I said that even before
I knew I was."* – *Muhammad Ali*

DATE:___/___/___

NEVER EVER GIVE UP

DATE:___/___/___

think positive

"Take chances, make mistakes. That's how you grow. Pain nourishes your courage. You have to fail in order to practice being brave." –
Mary Tyler Moore

DATE:___/___/___

MAKE IT HAPPEN

DATE:____/____/____

think positive

"If we're growing, we're always going to be out
of our comfort zone." – John C Maxwell

BELIEVE YOU CAN

DATE:___/___/___

think positive

"The will to win, the desire to succeed, the urge to reach your full potential... these are the keys that will unlock the door to personal excellence." – Confucius

BELIEVE IN YOURSELF

DATE:___/___/___

think
positive

"All you can change is yourself, but sometimes that changes everything!" – Gary W Goldstein

TAKE ACTION!

DATE:___/___/___

think
positive

"Success is not a destination but the consciousness of knowing that you
are enjoying what you are doing and by doing it every day you are
rewarded with great results." - Frank Mullani

NEVER EVER GIVE UP

DATE:___/___/___

think positive

DATE:___/___/___

MAKE IT HAPPEN

DATE:___/___/___

think
positive

"If you think you can do a thing or think you
can't do a thing, you're right." – Henry Ford

DATE:____/____/____

BELIEVE
YOU CAN

DATE:___/___/___

think positive

"We are all here for some special reason. Stop being a prisoner of your past. Become the architect of your future." – Robin Sharma

DATE:___/___/___

"If opportunity doesn't knock, build a door." – Milton Berle

DATE:___/___/___

think positive

"Life is a gift, and it offers us the privilege, opportunity, and
responsibility to give something back by becoming more." – Tony Robbins

DATE:_____/_____/_____

"The secret of getting ahead is getting started." – Mark Twain

TAKE ACTION!

DATE:___/___/___

think
positive

"Today is a new beginning, a chance to turn your failures into
achievements & your sorrows into so goods. No room for excuses."
– Joel Brown

DATE:___/___/___

NEVER EVER GIVE UP

DATE:___/___/___

think positive

"If you want light to come into your life, you
need to stand where it is shining." – Guy Finley

DATE:____/____/____

MAKE IT HAPPEN

DATE:___/___/___

*think
positive*

"*Happiness is an attitude. We either make ourselves miserable,
or happy and strong. The amount of work is the same.*" –
Francesca Reigler

DATE:___/___/___

BELIEVE YOU CAN

DATE:___/___/___

think positive

"Hope is a waking dream." – Aristotle

DATE:___/___/___

BELIEVE IN YOURSELF

DATE:___/___/___

think positive

"You yourself, as much as anybody in the entire universe, deserve your love and affection." – Buddha

DATE:___/___/___

TAKE ACTION!

DATE:___/___/___

think
positive

"I've had a lot of worries in my life, most of
which never happened" – Mark Twain

DATE:___/___/___

"It does not matter how slowly you go as long as you do not stop" – Confucius

NEVER EVER GIVE UP

DATE:___/___/___

think positive

"Learning is a gift. Even when pain is your teacher." – Maya Watson

DATE:___/___/___

MAKE IT HAPPEN

DATE:___/___/___

think positive

"I may not have gone where I intended to go, but I think I have ended up where I needed to be." – Douglas Adams

DATE:___/___/___

BELIEVE YOU CAN

DATE:___/___/___

think positive

"Our greatest weakness lies in giving up. The most certain way to succeed is always to try just one more time." – Thomas Edison

DATE:___/___/___

BELIEVE IN YOURSELF

DATE:___/___/___

think positive

"We don't see things as they are, we see them as we are." – Anaís Nin

DATE:___/___/___

TAKE ACTION!

DATE:___/___/___

think
positive

"The only place where your dream becomes impossible
is in your own thinking." – Robert H Schuller

DATE:___/___/___

"Hope is a waking dream." — *Aristotle*

DATE:___/___/___

think positive

"If you can dream it, then you can achieve it. You will get all you want in life if you help enough other people get what they want." – Zig Ziglar

DATE:___/___/___

MAKE IT HAPPEN

DATE:___/___/___

think
positive

"Success consists of going from failure to failure without loss of enthusiasm." – Winston Churchill

DATE:___/___/___

BELIEVE YOU CAN

DATE:___/___/___

think
positive

"An attitude of positive expectation is the mark of
the superior personality." – Brian Tracy

DATE:___/___/___

"Never, never, never give up." –
Winston Churchill

DATE:___/___/___

think positive

"If opportunity doesn't knock, build a door." – Milton Berle

DATE:___/___/___

TAKE ACTION!

DATE:___/___/___

think positive

"Believe in yourself! Have faith in your abilities! Without a humble but reasonable confidence in your own powers you cannot be successful or happy." – Norman Vincent Peale

DATE:___/___/___

NEVER EVER GIVE UP

DATE:___/___/___

think positive

"The way to get started is to quit talking and
begin doing." - Walt Disney

DATE:___/___/___

MAKE IT HAPPEN

DATE: ___/___/___

think positive

"Happiness is not something readymade. It comes from your own actions." - Dalai Lama

DATE:___/___/___

BELIEVE YOU CAN

DATE: ___/___/___

think positive

"Challenges are what make life interesting and overcoming them is what makes life meaningful." - Joshua J. Marine

DATE:___/___/___

BELIEVE IN YOURSELF

DATE:___/___/___

think positive

"It is never too late to be what you might have been." - George Eliot

DATE:____/____/____

TAKE ACTION!

DATE:___/___/___

think positive

"Life is what we make it, always has been, always will be." - Grandma Moses

DATE:_____/_____/_____

"Believe and act as if it were impossible to fail."

NEVER EVER GIVE UP

DATE:___/___/___

think
positive

"I am thankful for all of those who said NO to me. Its because of them I'm doing it myself." - Albert Einstein

DATE:___/___/___

MAKE IT HAPPEN

DATE:___/___/___

think positive

"Do what makes YOU happy." - Malcolm Matthews

DATE:___/___/___

BELIEVE YOU CAN

DATE:____/____/____

think positive

"The mind is everything. What you think you become." - Buddha

DATE:___/___/___

BELIEVE IN YOURSELF

DATE:____/____/____

"Whatever the mind of man can conceive and believe, it can achieve." – Napoleon Hill

BELIEVE IN YOURSELF

DATE:___/___/___

"We become what we think about." –
Earl Nightingale

DATE:___/___/___

TAKE ACTION!

DATE:___/___/___

"Life is 10% what happens to me and 90% of how I react to it." – *Charles Swindoll*

MAKE IT HAPPEN

DATE:___/___/___

think positive

DATE:___/___/___

think
positive

DATE:___/___/___

BELIEVE IN YOURSELF

"I am not a product of my circumstances. I am a product of my decisions." – Stephen Covey

DATE:___/___/___

"Whether you think you can or you think you can't, you're right." — Henry Ford

NEVER EVER GIVE UP

DATE:___/___/___

MAKE IT HAPPEN

DATE:___/___/___

think positive

CREATIVE JOURNALS
FACTORY

THANK YOU WE HOPE YOU LIKE YOUR NOTEBOOK - JOURNAL
PLEASE WRITE YOUR REVIEW, IT MEANS A LOT TO US!